Teach the Ch...
THE TRUE MEANING OF CHRISTMAS

A Beloved Christmas Legend

Revised and retold
by Jeanne W. Anderson
Illustrated by Amy L. Hintze

Good Mountain Home Publishing

Copyright© 2014 Jeanne W. Anderson for the text*
*There are many variations of this Christmas story which have been told over the generations. This copyright is for this version which includes the original poem, "The Symbols of Christmas."
Copyright© 2014 Amy L. Hintze for the illustrations
Copyright© 2014 Nicole Christensen for "The Symbols of Christmas" music
Book design by Ryan Anderson

All rights reserved

No part of this book may be reproduced without the written permission of
Good Mountain Home Publishing

To order additional copies of this book email:
goodmountainhome@gmail.com
or write to:
 671 Ridge Dr.
Alpine, UT 84004

This book is dedicated to my parents,

John and Marcell Weaver who read favorite stories to me when I was a child.

I first heard this story when my mom shared it at our family Christmas party many years ago. There have been several variations of this Christmas Legend told over the generations. I hope you and your little ones enjoy this version of

"Teach the Children the True Meaning of Christmas."

Special thanks to:

My Heavenly Father and Savior, Jesus Christ for the gift of Christmas to the world!

My husband, Steve, for his loving support of my hobby to write books for children,

My son, Ryan for his mastery of the computer to produce this book,

My friend, Amy, for her delightful art work,

My friend, Nicki and her children for the beautiful music,

And, of course, to Santa Claus C.B. who shares the Magic of Christmas with the children!

One week before Christmas, I had a surprise visitor. This is how it happened: I had just finished the household chores for the night and finally had all the children down in bed, when I heard a noise in the front living room of our home. As I walked into the room, to my surprise, Santa Claus stepped out from behind the Christmas tree! He placed his finger over his lips, warning me to not cry out and wake the children.

I quietly asked, "Santa, what are you doing here?" I was concerned as I saw that Santa had tears in his eyes. His usual, jolly manner was gone.

Santa then quietly whispered a simple statement,

"Teach The Children."

I was puzzled; what did he mean? Anticipating my question, he brought forth a small toy bag from behind the tree. As I stood there, bewildered, Santa said again,

"Teach the children; teach them the true meaning of Christmas, the meaning that so many, busy people now-a-days seem to have forgotten!"

Santa then reached into his little bag and pulled out a small Green Fir Tree and placed it on the fireplace mantle. He said,

"Teach the children that the pure green color of the stately fir tree remains green all year round, depicting the everlasting hope of mankind. All the needles point Heavenward, making it a symbol of man's thoughts turning toward Heaven."

Next, Santa pulled a beautiful, Red Ornament from his bag and placed it on the tree.

"Teach the children that the red ornament displays the main color of Christmas. The color red reminds us of the Savior's blood. Christ gave his life and shed his blood that every one might have the gift of eternal life."

A brilliant Star was brought forth and placed at the top of the little tree.

"Teach the children that the star was the Heavenly sign of promise long ago. God promised a Savior for the world, and the star was a sign of the fulfillment of that promise."

Santa then reached into his bag and pulled out a red Candle to place on the tree.

"Teach the children that the candle symbolizes that Christ is the Light of the World. When we see this light, we are reminded that we should share His gospel light with others."

A lovely, round Wreath was removed from his bag. Santa carefully placed the little wreath on the tree.

"Teach the children that the wreath symbolizes the eternal nature of love. Real love never ceases. Love is one continuous round of affection."

Next came a red and white, striped Candy Cane which Santa hung on the tree.

"Teach the children that the candy cane represents the shepherd's crook. The crook on the staff helps to bring the sheep that have strayed back to the fold. The candy cane is the symbol that we should be our brother's keeper."

Santa brought forth a precious Angel ornament from his bag and said,

"Teach the children that the angels heralded in the glorious news of the Savior's birth. The angels sang, Glory to God in the highest, and on earth peace, good will toward men."

I was deep in thought when I heard a little twinkling sound. Santa was softly ringing a tiny, gold Bell as he said,

"Teach the children that the sound of a bell is used to call the wandering sheep back to the fold; likewise, the bell reminds mankind to return to the fold of the Savior, our Good Shepherd."

*N*ow, Santa pulled a small wrapped Gift from his bag.

"Teach the children that God so loved the world that He gave His only begotten Son. God's gift to mankind is eternal life, made possible through the atonement of our Savior, Jesus Christ. The Wise Men knelt before Baby Jesus and presented him with gifts of gold, frankincense, and myrrh. We give gifts to each other to show this same Spirit of Love."

The gift was tied with a beautiful red Bow.

"Teach the children that the bow symbolizes that we should all be tied together in the bonds of love and goodwill."

Santa placed the gift under the little Christmas tree.

As Santa looked at the little decorated tree on the mantel, he seemed pleased. I saw a smile on his face, and the twinkle had returned to his eyes.

Tears now came to my eyes, as I felt my heart filled with the true Spirit of Christmas. "Thank you, Santa," I whispered;

"I will teach the children the true meaning of Christmas, the full story of what Christmas is really all about."

I hesitated, and then I asked, "What about you though, Santa? You have always been such a delightful part of the Christmas Season."

Santa placed a little red elf hat on the tree, winked and replied,

"Well now, Mrs. Claus, my reindeer, the elves, and I symbolize the Magic of the Christmas Season! This magic is all part of the goodwill and generosity we feel because of the True Meaning and Spirit of Christmas.

The final item Santa gently pulled from his sack was a beautifully crafted, little Figurine of Baby Jesus. He held it out for me to see, and then tenderly placed it on the mantel under the tree.

Santa then turned to me and said,

"For unto you is born this day, a Saviour, which is Christ the Lord."

"This little figurine reminds us that Christmas is the day we celebrate the birth of Baby Jesus."

"Please, teach the children to say their prayers, read the scriptures, and to always be kind to others. Following the example of Jesus will help all of us to keep the Spirit of Christmas in our hearts forever."

I slowly shut my eyes to think on all that Santa had taught me. It was just for a moment, but when I opened them again, Santa was gone!

> I pondered and wondered and thrilled with delight,
> As I sat and viewed all these symbols at night.
> I dozed as I sat in the soft candle light,
> And my thoughts were of Santa, and all he made right.
> To give and to help, to love and to serve,
> Are the best things of life, all men can deserve.
> Now Santa Claus, as the jolly, old elf,
> Gave the best meaning of Christmas itself.
> It's the sign of the gift of love and of life,
> The ending of evil, the ceasing of strife.
> His message to me on this pre-Christmas night,
> Has opened a treasure of deepest insight:
> We must follow the Savior in all that we do,
> To the cause of His Gospel, we must always be true.

Teach the Children the True Meaning of Christmas

Fir Tree: The green shows everlasting life, the needles point heavenward.

Red Ornament: Displays the main color of Christmas representing the Savior's blood which was shed for us.

Star: A heavenly sign of prophecy of the Savior's birth.

Candle: Symbolizes that Christ is the Light of the World; we should share His Gospel light.

Wreath: The eternal nature of love; one continuous round of affection.

Candy Cane: The shepherd's crook used to bring lambs back into the fold; a reminder that we are all our brother's keepers.

Angels: Heralded in the glorious news of the Savior's birth.

Bell: Rings out to guide lost sheep back to the fold; all mankind should return to the fold of the Savior, our Good Shepherd.

Gift: God gave us the greatest gift of his Son. The Wise Men brought gifts to Baby Jesus. We should give gifts in the same spirit of love.

Gift Bow: We should all be tied together in the bonds of love and goodwill.

Santa, Mrs. Claus, the Reindeer, and Elves: All symbolize the Christmas MAGIC we feel because of the goodwill and Spirit of the Christmas Season.

Figurine of Baby Jesus: A reminder of what Christmas is all about! Follow the example of Jesus to keep the Spirit of Christmas always in our hearts.

THE SYMBOLS OF CHRISTMAS

The STAR is the Heavenly sign.

The WREATH shows continuous love.

The BABY JESUS, a birth divine,

Is a GIFT from our Father above.

RED DECOR on a GREEN FIR TREE,

The colors of eternal life.

Christ shed His blood so that all can see

His atonement for evil and strife.

The CANDY is the shepherd's CANE

To bring back the wandering fold.

The ANGELS taught that all would gain

The prophecy of old.

The GIFT BOW ties us all as one.

The BELL rings out in the night

Leading to the Father and the Son,

Is the CANDLE of Christmas, God's Light.

Poem written by Jeanne W. Anderson for Christmas 2014

Recipe for Holly Berry Christmas Cookies

½ Cup butter or margarine

4 Cups miniature marshmallows or 40 large marshmallows

One teaspoon vanilla

One teaspoon liquid green food coloring

(a few drops is not enough; use a full teaspoon of coloring)

5 Cups corn flakes

Small red hot cinnamon candies

1. Spray a large baking sheet with non-stick cooking spray.

2. Melt the butter and marshmallows together in a large pan by stirring constantly on medium heat. When melted, remove from heat and add the vanilla and green food coloring. Stir until well blended. Add the corn flakes and stir until all corn flakes are well coated.

3. Place a large spoonful of the corn flake mixture on the baking sheet to form a little holly mound. It will be helpful if you spray a little of the cooking spray on your spoon. Let a child help you to place three red hot candies on each cookie to be the holly berries. Work fairly quickly to place and form the holly mounds before the mixture hardens. Make one batch at a time; do not try to double the recipe as it will harden too quickly.

4. Let cool at room temperature or in the refrigerator.

Makes 24 cookies

You will know if anyone has "stolen" a cookie off the plate prematurely becuase the culprit will have a green tongue!

About the Story Teller

Jeanne Anderson and her husband, Steve, currently reside in Alpine, Utah. They are the parents of five boys; thus, they have served as Boy Scout Leaders for over 20 years. Their family has grown to include five beautiful daughters that have married into the family. At the time of this writing, they have seven darling grandchildren with two more on the way! Jeanne has a Bachelor's Degree from Brigham Young University in Social Work. She loves gardening, all sports, being in the mountains, and writing stories for children. She is a 25 year volunteer with the Festival of Trees, a charity to help needy children at Primary Children's Hospital. If you would like to reach Jeanne or to order additional copies of this book, please contact her at goodmountainhome@gmail.com. She would love to hear from you!

About the Illustrator

Amy Hintze graduated from Brigham Young University with a Bachelor of Fine Arts degree in Illustration. In addition to drawing and painting for books and magazines, Amy is pursuing a degree in motherhood, with three adorable boys and two adorable girls. She has also enjoyed illustrating the Mormon Tabernacle Choir's Music and the Spoken Word broadcast since 2007. In her nonexistent spare time she enjoys being in the outdoors, listening to music, yoga , teaching art, and spending quality time with her wonderfully supportive husband, Brian. Amy met Jeanne when her small family moved to Alpine in 2000. Amy currently resides with her rambunctious family in Lindon, Utah. See more of her artwork or request artwork prints at amyhintzeart.blogspot.com

The Symbols of Christmas

1. The star is the Heav-en-ly sign, The wreath shows con-tin-u-ous love. The bab-y Je-sus, a birth Di-vine is a gift from our Fa-ther a-
2. The can-dy is the shep-herds cane To bring back the wan-der-ing fold. The an-gels taught that all would gain the pro-phe-cy of

Words: Jeanne W. Anderson, 2014
Music: Nicole Christensen, 2014

Teach the Children
THE TRUE MEANING OF CHRISTMAS

Santa has come to visit with a desire to "Teach the Children the True Meaning of Christmas." Santa explains the meaning of the candy cane, star, wreath and all the symbols of Christmas which turn our hearts to the Christ Child. This beloved Christmas legend has been enjoyed by families over the generations. Storyteller Jeanne W. Anderson and artist Amy L. Hintze have teamed with Santa to present this delightful illustrated story to add to your family Christmas book collection.

Good Mountain Home Publishing

Made in the USA
Coppell, TX
20 December 2021